Jesus Has

Delivered

You

(now what?)

By James M. Thayer

For the children of God,

Christ has called you into freedom; now walk in His victory.

Seek First Productions, LLC
- Established 2012

ISBN: 979-8-9877867-4-1

Contents

Introduction

As a healing evangelist in the service of Jesus I have seen Him free hundreds of people from demonic bondage - ranging from debilitating depression and panic attacks all the way through sicknesses that must have been manufactured in the bowels of hell such as akinesia, dystonia, and ehlers danlos syndrome.

I have also, unfortunately, seen dozens of people reshackled by our enemy within weeks of being liberated.

This booklet is for the person who has recently encountered the Lord of Glory and found themselves free from the chains they formerly carried. I wrote it so you might maintain your freedom.

Your Freedom

"When the unclean spirit has gone out of a person, it passes through waterless places seeking rest, but finds none. Then it says, 'I will return to my house from which I came.' And when it comes, it finds the house empty, swept, and put in order. Then it goes and brings with it seven other spirits more evil than itself, and they enter

and dwell there, and the last
state of that person is worse
than the first."
– Matthew 12:43-45

This verse is often glossed over
because it seems randomly
placed within the context of a
larger point Jesus is trying to
make, but it is a dire warning for
us all. We know that when Jesus
frees us from demonic oppres-
sion, He does it by the Finger of
God which is the Holy Spirit
(Luke 11:20). Matthew 12:43-45

tells us what happens next – the evil spirit is displaced and goes through dry places without rest. It then tries to reclaim its old "home" by recruiting other demons more wicked than itself to brute force, or more often *deceive*, its way back in.

Understand the spirit considers us a home, a place of refuge and rest where it can be satiated. You must look at these things like parasites which don't want to be discovered, and certainly don't want to be removed. Once removed, they desperately try to enter again.

When they come back, will they find an empty home as this passage states? Or will they find one full of the Holy Spirit and clothed in the armor of God? It is vital we don't merely empty our home of sickness, lies, and darkness, but be filled with the light of Christ – His truth, His life, and His Spirit.

The number one mistake I see people make at this juncture is to not expect a counterattack from our enemy. Expect it because Jesus said it would happen, but do not fear it.

Counterattack

"So if the Son sets you
free, you will be free indeed."
– John 8:36

This verse is a promise from
God. If Jesus has set you free,
then you are free. Understand
this promise and stand on it no
matter what Satan presents to
you. He will try to fool you into
believing you were not actually

healed or not actually freed, and
if you give into his lies over the
truth of God found in this bible
verse, he will be able to re-
shackle you again with your for-
mer affliction.

Practically, this is how it can
play out. Pretend you were freed
from debilitating depression.
Someone prayed over you, you
felt it lift, and maybe you would
even say you felt "lighter." Two
days later you wake up and im-
mediately feel gloomy. You

might even hear voices speaking to you such as, "You weren't actually freed; you will always be depressed; see, even God can't help you, etc."

In that moment you have a choice: either agree with your feelings and thoughts, or agree with the Word of God. In the West we have such a tendency to take evidence into account and form a conclusion based on it.

"Are your symptoms of disease back? That must mean you are still sick."

It sounds *very* convincing, but it is a lie.

Note: Keep in mind, I'm writing to the person who was actually freed and healed for a time. If your symptoms never left to begin with, then this book can't apply to your situation.

The bible tells us to "submit to God, resist the devil, and he will flee (James 4:7)." It is vital that we do the first part if we want to see the second part. *Submit to God.* That means no matter what you feel or think, you are going to trust Jesus over yourself or your enemy.

A friend told me a story once of a woman who was healed from terrible physical affliction in a moment. She felt the power of God rush through her and all her symptoms left. She was freed!

But one day the symptoms returned. In that moment she called my friend and told him, "All of my symptoms have returned. I do not know what is going on, all I know is I am healed."

The symptoms lingered for a while, but eventually they left again and never came back. This woman stood on the word of

God despite what she was being presented by Satan.

When Satan returns, he tries to prod and poke. He wants to test your resolve – to sift you. Do you actually believe Jesus, or will you be deceived and allow him back into your life? The moment you agree with him is when he comes back and digs in deeper.

I was once afflicted by an evil spirit which caused me such great pain it sent me to the ER.

Doctors could not diagnose it –
I basically had symptoms of
three or four different diagnosis,
but the symptoms did not align
to narrow any one of them
down.

My wife and my co-worker in
the gospel, along with an inter-
cessor, prayed over me. I
coughed violently, and the next
thing I knew I was free. All my
pain left! I went about my busi-
ness for the next week and a half
when, suddenly, the symptoms

returned. This time they were not as bad, but still awful. Again my wife prayed over me, I coughed violently, and was delivered by Jesus.

About a week later I felt the symptoms coming on faintly. I reached out to one of my intercessors (people who pray for my ministry) and asked her to inquire on the Lord for me about my situation. She responded that all she was hearing was to "stand steadfast in the Lord."

"Therefore put on the full armor of God, so that when the day of evil comes, you may be able to stand your ground, and after you have done everything, to stand." – Ephesians 6:13

I did exactly that. The entire day I did my best to ignore the physical feeling in my body and I kept praying to the Lord, "I stand on your word, I have been freed, I am healed."

The faint issue never amounted to anything greater and by nightfall it left me. Satan came to test me, but I rejected his word for the sake of the Word of God.

Defenses

"Be sober-minded; be watchful. Your adversary the devil prowls around like a roaring lion, seeking someone to devour."
– 1 Peter 5:8

Lions do not typically go after the gazelle in the middle of the herd. They attack the one outside the herd with limited

protection from the group.
More than any other trait, the
people I see freed by Jesus sadly
reshackled are the ones not in a
church. When I was under attack, and then later counterat-
tacked, notice I had several people in my church and family to
turn to. Jesus used them to de-
liver me and to remind me that I
needed to stand on God's prom-
ises.

Being planted in a church is vital for Christian sustainability
and growth. Paul said the body

of Christ was made up of various members like those of a human body – and that one body part couldn't tell another body part "I don't need you" because we need all members working in unity (1 Cor 12:12-27).

Do not miss that first church meeting after your deliverance. When you go, praise God for what He has done for you and get involved with believers there. Ask them to pray for you to be able to sustain any counterattack the enemy has planned, and allow them to strengthen you when needed like Aaron and Hur did for Moses to win their battle (Exodus 17:12-14)

We have already discussed the importance of standing on the truth of God's word, but I want to drive home the point that you need to be reading the bible. Deliverance isn't so much about driving out darkness as it is about pouring light in.

"So Jesus said to the Jews who had believed him, "If you abide in my word, you are truly my disciples, and you will know the truth, and the truth will set you free (John 8:31-32)."

Ask yourself why the spirit was able to enter in the first place. Was it because of habitual sin? Unforgiveness and bitterness? Trauma you endured? Mindsets you developed such as unworthiness or self-hatred? Did you give into condemnation and shame? Did you agree that you'd never be healed?

Whatever the doorway was, delve into the Word of God and begin to replace the lies you formerly believed, or actions you formally committed, with truth. At the end of this book, I will give you some suggested scripture to reflect on based on what your previous mindset may have been.

Do not neglect the secret place. Jesus taught us how we should pray. He said we should go into our rooms, shut the door, and pray to God in secret. Jesus said the Father would be there (Matthew 6:6). Most of your Christian walk will be empowered from secret prayer time when no one else is around. This is where you will encounter the glory of God washing over you and He will draw you deeper and deeper into Himself.

Whereas you once were familiar with an unclean spirit, the secret place is where you will become familiar with the Holy Spirit of God. The bible tells us to commune with Him – to talk with Him. He will guide you and He will comfort you.

After you were delivered, a minister should have prayed for God to fill you with the Holy Spirit. For example, if you were freed from panic attacks, the minister should have prayed for the peace of God to fill its place. If this did not happen, simply ask the Father to fill you while you are praying in the secret place.

In addition to getting involved at a church, studying scripture, and praying in the secret place, I also advise you to study your authority in Christ.

In Luke 10, Jesus sends out 72 disciples to preach the good news and heal the sick. When they return, they tell Jesus a marvelous discovery – that even the demons submitted to them in Jesus' name.

"He replied, 'I saw Satan fall like lightning from heaven. I

have given you authority to trample on snakes and scorpions and to overcome all the power of the enemy; nothing will harm you. However, do not rejoice that the spirits submit to you, but rejoice that your names are written in heaven.'" – Luke 10:18-20

If you are a follower of Jesus you have authority over demons. Do you believe Him when He tells you this? Know that it is true, and when that spirit returns to take back its old "home," verbally, out loud, tell it to leave. This can be a very simple command such as, "Spirit of lust, leave me now, I've been freed by Jesus" or "Spirit of sickness, go now, in Jesus' name, I have been healed."

You will sometimes even feel the unclean spirit lifting off you – like a tingly sensation leaving your body. Use the authority Jesus has given you the moment you feel a symptom return. Do not wait, and do not give up until it has lifted. If it isn't going easily, ask people in your church to pray for you.

If the spirit entered through witchcraft, ask the Holy Spirit what objects in your home He desires you to throw away or burn. Get rid of anything remotely related to witchcraft, new age, or paganism – even if it is expensive or was a gift given to you.

If the spirit entered through habitual sin, do not engage in that sin any longer.

"See, you are well again. Stop sinning or something worse may happen to you." – John 5:14

Victory

Victory was won at the cross of Christ. When a minister prayed for you to be delivered, all he or she did was apply what Christ procured for you by the power of the Holy Spirit. That victory is endless. Even if the battle comes back to your doorstep, understand the war is won in Jesus.

"In all these things we are more than conquerors through

him who loved us." – Romans 8:37

You are a conqueror, not a victim. Fight with every aspect of the armor of God – truth, faith, the gospel message, the sword of the Spirit, etc. Jesus has achieved victory, so now we apply it and maintain it using the resources He has provided us.

One more note: If the spirit comes back and gains entry even if you tried your best to stand on the Word of God -

don't take condemnation or shame along with the affliction. Submit to God, resist, and don't hesitate to ask a deliverance minister to pray for you again!

Bible Verses

As I previously mentioned, I encourage you to replace lies you may have believed, even since childhood, with the truth of God's word. We must stop believing what our parents, spouse, or abusers have said about us. We must stop believing what Satan or we ourselves have told us. Instead, we now must believe what God has spoken over our lives.

Unworthiness
John 3:16, Hebrews 12:2 (you were the joy!), Romans 8:15

Self-Hatred
1 Corinthians 6:19-20, Romans 8:1, 1 John 1:9

Trauma
Psalm 34:17-20, Matthew 12:20, Isaiah 61:1

Unforgiveness/Bitterness
Matthew 18:21-35, Matthew 6:15, Matthew 5:7

Sin/Witchcraft
Romans 6:1-7, Deuteronomy 18:10-11

Shame
Job 11:14-19, Isaiah 54:4-5, 1 John 3:20, Philippians 1:6, Luke 15:3-7

Fear/Anxiety
2 Timothy 1:7, Joshua 1:9, Psalm 46:1-3, Psalm 23:4, Philippians 4:6